Leadership Truths
One Story at a Time

Terry Paulson, PhD

First Edition
Amber Eagle Press, Agoura Hills, California

Published by: **Amber Eagle Press**
Post Office Box 365, Agoura Hills, CA 91376-0365
http://www.terrypaulson.com
info@terrypaulson.com

Printed in the United States of America

ISBN Print Edition: 1-878077-00-7 (978-1-878077-00-4)
ISBN Large Print Edition: 1-878077-06-6 (978-1-878077-06-6)
ISBN AdobeReader.PDF Edition: 1-878077-01-5 (978-1-878077-01-1)
ISBN MisrosoftReader.LIT Edition: 1-878077-02-3 (978-1-878077-02-8)
ISBN: PalmeReader.PDB Edition: 1-878077-03-1 (978-1-878077-03-5)
ISBN: MobiPocketReader.PRC Edition: 1-878077-05-8 (978-1-878077-05-9)

Library of Congress Control Number: 2006905819
Paulson, Terry
Leadership truths one story at a time/Terry Paulson.

TABLE OF CONTENTS

Acknowledgments

To individually cite and thank all of the people involved in the stories included in this book would require more space than is available, but this book would not be possible without them. I thank them all for sharing my life's journey in some meaningful way. Some I experienced directly. Others came secondhand, but all have impacted me as I hope they will impact you.

A special thanks goes to my parents, Ann and Homer Paulson, whose strong faith, values and patriotism helped shape my own. The same goes for my loving wife, Lorie, and my son, Sean. Both have shared my passion for life and an appreciation for good stories. All of them have been great humor consumers; they love to laugh and learn!

I sincerely thank Dan Poynter of Para Publishing for his encouragement and publishing acumen, Claudia Volkman for her timely, professional editing, layout and design work, Creative Factory Inc.'s Abel Robinson for his vibrant and effective cover design, Emil Ozkan for the cover photo images and Lightning Source and Rosetta Machine for their help in launching into the ebook world.

Introduction

"Day after day we seek an answer to the ageless question Aristotle posed in Ethics: 'How should a human being lead his life?' But the answer eludes us, hiding behind a blur of racing hours as we struggle to fit our means to our dreams, fuse idea with passion, turn desire into reality. We're swept along on a risk-ridden shuttle through time.... As our faith in traditional ideologies diminishes, we turn to the source we still believe in: the art of story." –Robert McKee

My father used to tuck my brother and me into bed every night. We'd say our prayers, and then he would tell us a story of his days on the farms of Illinois. He'd tell stories of overcoming hardships and heroic stories about his pony, Patches. Over the years, I came to know most of his stories. As the oldest child, he sometimes would start the story and then ask me to complete it. That started my life as a storyteller. As a psychologist and professional speaker, I've been telling stories every since.

"In recent years, social scientists have come to appreciate what political, religious, and military figures have long known: that stories constitute a uniquely powerful currency in human relationships... And I suggest,

further, that it is stories...of identity—narratives that help individuals think about and feel who they are, where they come from, and where they are headed— that constitute the single most powerful weapon in the leader's...arsenal." –Howard Gardner

Story is what penetrates. People remember stories more easily than they ever remember a numbing list of abstract teaching points. After all, when was the last data slide or graph that you remember as the highlight of a talk?

Good stories unlock those seldom-used mental doors and lead the listener through their own house of memories. Those memories, once triggered, allow people to experience themselves, their lives, and their memories in a fresh way. It prompts the listener to say, "I can see it happening!" "I've been there!" or "It could happen to me!" When they connect a shared story with their own life's experience, they retain the story and the point whenever they think of that experience.

In my years of speaking on topics ranging from assertiveness to listening, from leadership to optimism, I've found that not every story is worth telling. But some stories work over and over again with audiences everywhere. I treasure those stories.

I always want my audiences to say, "What a great story worth remembering!" not just "What a great storyteller!" When told well, my stories bring wisdom alive for my audiences. I hope they serve you as well.

"We cannot light the fire, we cannot speak the prayers, we do not know the place, but we can tell the story of how it was done. The holy teachers were right: telling a story is a kind of prayer, a kind of meditation, a sacred act. It makes magic happen." –Erica Jong

This book is a collection of some of my favorite leadership stories. For over thirty years as a professional speaker, I have used these stories to touch audiences and impact their lives. So, come with me now through my unique window to the world of work through the power of story.

What's Working for You?

"People need leadership to help them maintain their focus on the tough questions. Disciplined attention is the currency of leadership." — *Ronald Heifetz*

When I was seventeen, I helped build the mile-long electron microscope at the Stanford Linear Accelerator in Palo Alto, California. My job title that summer was "lab technician." I drove a truck. I didn't know why they called me a "lab technician," but now I'm sure it was for funding purposes.

No matter what the title, I worked hard for three months as part of an eight-man construction team. This was my first big job, and I was proud to be part of the team. I was open to all the possibilities that venturing into the real world of work can conjure up. I had previously spent some time working on a family farm in Illinois and had also picked apricots by the hour, but now I had an actual job title. I was also being paid well enough that I could afford to go out. Now, that was progress.

As with most memorable events, it's the people, not the work, that we remember. That summer was no exception. I got to meet Jack Nichols, the best supervisor I've ever worked for. Long before anyone talked about *empowering leadership* or related fads, Jack lived empowerment.

Jack had a statement on his wall that I will never forget. I'm not sure who said it first, but since it was on Jack's wall, I will give him the credit. The sign read: "Every person I work with knows something better than I. My job is to listen long enough to find it and use it."

Jack *literally* walked his talk. Every week he took a fifteen-minute walk with each of his direct subordinates. Even as his only summer employee, I was expected to join him for a walk every Friday. What impressed me most

> *"Every person I work with knows something better than I. My job is to listen long enough to find it and use it."*

was that during our walks he seldom did much talking; Jack preferred to invest his time in listening. And it was the questions he repeatedly asked that fostered a pivotal emotional learning experience in my young life.

The question that had the biggest impact on me was the first question he asked. Jack liked to get right to the point. His words hung in the air as we walked, "Terry, you've been working here a week; what's working for you?"

Of all the questions he could have asked, he had to pick one I had no ready answer for. You don't ask teens, "What's working for you?" You ask them: "How is it going in school?" "Are you scoring any touchdowns?" and even, "Are you on drugs?"

I was usually quick with good answers, but this one

question took me more than a few uncomfortable moments of searching for anything worth saying. I finally replied tentatively, "I know the equipment is very sensitive, so the guys taught me how to load the truck. That's been working."

Jack seemed glad that I was learning from the team, but his next sentence was a surprise. He said thoughtfully, "When I first met you, Terry, I knew that there was something special about you. In fact, I expect to learn something from *you* this summer. To do that, I'm going to ask you this question every Friday."

I couldn't believe his words! Had this man forgotten what it was like to be a teenager? I, like other teens, did what adults told me to do. I was good at taking tests and giving back the answers the adults told me to learn. Didn't he know that the guys I was working with weren't going to give me a new idea to share with him every week? This guy had to be crazy! I was sure that if he could just talk to my mother, she would confirm that I didn't know anything of value. She might even write me an excuse note!

Jack ruined my summer! Instead of just doing a job, he made me think...every week! But like any good student, I went to the only authority model I knew: teachers. I had done well in school by learning how teachers gave tests. I studied everything for the first test, but once I had passed that test, I could learn the teacher's test paradigm. If the tests covered only class notes, I just scanned the text and focused my study on the notes.

Jack helped me learn an important lesson about

leadership that summer. Jack taught me that, just like teachers, leaders are known by the questions they consistently ask. Jack's question was "What's working for you?" He didn't give me the answer; he wanted me to come up with my own. I had to think differently about what I was doing.

That summer, my best day was always Thursday. If nothing had worked by Thursday, I had a mission! Something had to work, because my walk with Jack was Friday and he was going to ask me that stupid question. I always had something to share on Friday, and Jack always listened.

In retrospect, I can see that Jack knew how to get the best out of his team. He was not particularly charismatic, but he came alive as a listener. He was more excited about my ideas than he was about his own. He would ask questions to expand my thinking. He would nod his

Jack's question was "What's working for you?"
He didn't give me the answer; he wanted me
to come up with my own.

approval, even encourage me to take my answers further. I'm sure some of my ideas were a bit bizarre, but he always treated them with thoughtful dignity.

Twice that summer, he asked me if I would mind if he shared my idea with the team at one of our staff meetings. I agreed, at the same time trying to hide my excitement behind an appropriate amount of macho indifference. At that first meeting, I thought he had forgotten my idea. Then, halfway through the staff meeting, he said, "Terry came up with something the other day. In fact, he did such a good job of explaining it to me... Terry, why don't you tell the men what you told me?"

My heart raced. Panic! *No, this is not good! I'm a kid; these people are old...at least thirty or thirty-one!* But Jack's reassuring eyes and warm smile calmed me. I looked only at him as I shared my idea.

We changed procedures twice that summer as a result of my input. I felt special, but it did not make me special. It did, however, make Jack very special as a leader, because he did the same for each member of the team.

As Jack walked me to the car on my last day that summer, he said, "Terry, I told you when you started this summer that I was going to learn something from you. We all did. You're going to go far. Now, if you ever need a job, you come back. I'd hire you in minute."

I went into my senior year of high school on a high. I had made a difference in the real world. I had also inherited a mentor who to this day helps inspire and guide my actions as a leader.

Our world of work tends to focus on problems. The questions leaders ask often reflect that preoccupation: "What's wrong?" "Got any problems?" "What, no problems? Then get back to work!"

Jack lived his leadership by helping his team look

for opportunities. He didn't push his team; he helped us soar on the wings of our own ideas.

As a leader, you too are known by the questions you consistently ask. Okay, you knew I was going to ask! What's working for you? What role can you play in mentoring others to enable them to see the contributions they can make to your organization?

You deserve to know *the rest of the story.* Eighteen years after reporting to Jack, I had the pleasure of presenting

As a leader, you too are kown by the questions you consistently ask.

to him at a University of California at Berkeley extension program. There were nearly 400 managers from different companies in attendance, and I did not see that Jack was one of them until fifteen minutes into my program when our eyes met.

I had not seen him in eighteen years. I had even forgotten his name, but I remembered his face. Now, it was my turn to get even! He had embarrassed me in front of eight men at that staff meeting. I was going to get to get even with him in front of 400 people.

I looked at him and said, "There you are!" It was like his face had come off a milk carton. He had that "deer in the headlights" look in his eyes. Suddenly it hit me. He didn't remember who I was. My mentor had forgotten me!

"I reported to you at the Stanford Linear Accelerator,"

I said, slowly trying to gather the facts that would jar his memory. "It was the summer of 1963."

Suddenly, he remembered. Either that, or he was frightened and thought he'd better pretend that he remembered. To let him know that I had also forgotten, I asked him for his name.

In front of 400 people, I got to tell Jack what I didn't know as a seventeen-year-old teenager.

"You were the best supervisor I ever worked for," I said with authentic appreciation. I then told the audience the story you have just read.

He was a humble man. You could tell he was uncomfortable with public praise, but he came up to me at the break. We talked for an extended time about old memories and new adventures.

"I just wanted to thank you for what you said," Jack finally shared.

"I meant every word of it," I replied.

"What would the alumni of your leadership say about how you impacted their lives?"

"I know. As a manager, you don't get to hear from too many of your alumni," Jack said with a smile. "It's very satisfying to know that you can make a difference. I'm proud to have been part of your life's story."

If you aren't touched by this story, get out of leadership. One of our primary jobs as leaders is to leave people better off for having worked for us.

Now, what would the alumni of your leadership say about how you impacted their lives?

His Keeper System Was a Keeper!

"The most important part of the meeting is immediately after. What are they going to do with it once it is over?" – Walter Hailey

It was during the first break of a full-day program that he approached me with an endearing compliment, "I'm really enjoying your program."

"Thank you," I replied. "You can stay." We both laughed.

"I would like to ask you a question," he continued. "You talked about the importance of lifelong learning, and I agree. Do you attend programs yourself?"

Do you walk your talk? I thought. "That's a legitimate question," I replied. "I do. I attend other programs on topics I speak on. I like to see what others are doing to bring topics alive. I also get ongoing training at the American Society for Training and Development and attend presentations on speaking at the National Speakers Association."

"Good, that sounds exciting," he continued. "Do you take notes?"

I now knew this was a test, but at least I felt I was doing well so far. I answered confidently, "Yes, I always take notes. To a fault, I am a compulsive note taker."

"What do you do with your notes?" He pursued his train of thought with enthusiasm.

His questions were getting tougher. I replied, "I have a very organized filing system. I write in the top right corner of my notes the name of the file they belong in, and then I put them in a pile to be filed. That way I know that I can get to those notes when I need them."

I felt rather proud of my own answer.

His pursuit continued. "In the past week, how many times have you reviewed past notes from seminars you have attended?"

Now I was beginning to get a bit uncomfortable. I paused, scanning my memory of my past week hoping to find some evidence of a review. Unable to find any

"In the past week, how many times have you reviewed past notes from seminars you have attended?"

evidence of this, my mind raced to research I had read earlier in my career indicating that within four days of a seminar there is a 70% drop in retention. But if there was a review of the content learned in those four days, there was a 40% *increase* in retention.

"I had a very busy week," I confessed.

He refused to let me escape. He pushed further, "I can understand having a busy week. I will give you a month. How many times in the last month have you reviewed past training seminars?"

"Why are you putting me through this pain?" I asked,

smiling at his friendly assault on my credibility. "I wanted to tell you what I do to make sure I review my notes," he confessed. "You could have just told me," I said laughing. "You didn't have to put me through all this!"

Then again, sometimes good questions peel back our resistance, opening us up to our own need for change. He made me uncomfortable, but he left me open to an idea that to this day I continue to use.

"What do you do to ensure your review?" I asked.

"I keep what I call *Keeper Notes*," he promptly replied. "I limit my self to one page of notes that I want to keep for review. If I can't write on two sides of one piece of paper the key insights and action items that I plan on reviewing, I probably won't review it."

"How much do you write?"

"I try to limit my entries to one sentence for each item," he continued. "I try to capture the main thought. By reading that line, my brain does the review of the rest of the concept. I don't write down things I already do. I don't write down things I know I won't do. I just write down and review my *Keepers!*"

"How do you make sure you review them instead of just stockpile them?"

"I put my *Keeper Notes* in a notebook that I place next to my phone," he said with a smile. "The only time I review them is when I'm on hold on the telephone. I grab my notebook, go to the next page and review the notes. I often can review an entire page in the time I'm waiting. I review all my notes five times a year, just using my hold time."

"What a great use of time!"

"There is a cost," he confessed. "I usually forget who I am talking to. I just say, 'I'm sorry, I have forgotten your name, but let me tell you something important!' They laugh and forgive me."

The conversation ended as quickly as it had begun, but I shared his strategy with those in attendance. Even more importantly, I put his suggestion into practice. Soon, I too was reviewing my own *Keeper Notes*.

The only problem was that I was seldom at my desk. At the suggestion of a sales representative who had adapted a *Keeper System* to fit his mobile lifestyle, I took my lists and recorded them, first onto a cassette tape and now onto a CD. I record ten key statements, add some of my favorite music, and then add more *Keepers*.

"The only time I review my Keeper Notes is when I'm on hold on the telephone."

I even had fun adding my own LA traffic reports to the recordings — "You know the traffic is lousy! Just keep driving." My commutes became focused time for my *Keeper* review.

I have no name to attach to the origin of this great *Keeper Strategy*, only an enduring habit that I have shared with thousands of other program participants over the years. You see, it isn't the number of "happy face" evaluations or standing ovations you receive as a speaker that counts in the great game of business. It's the difference

What's worth keeping and reviewing from your favorite books and training experiences?

you make in people's behavior and attitudes months after the program has faded into mere memories.

That participant made a difference for me. And I hope this story is a *Keeper* for you. You might start by identifying, storing, reviewing and sharing the *Keepers* you pick up from this book!

The Prairie Farm Consultant

"I've been guided in my work by the notion that older is often better. If an idea has been around for a few thousand years, it's been submitted to many tests—which is a good indicator that it might have some real merit. We're fixated on newness, which often misleads us into elevating novelty over substance." –Debahish Chatterjee

Farming had been Harvey Swanson's life. He'd played the good hands, and he'd weathered the bad hands God had dealt him in his 87-year struggle with the land. As a young teen visiting from the big city, I had spent time with Harvey on trips to the farm country. Both my parents were 100% Swedish—all Paulsons, Carlsons, Swansons, and Petersons. They grew up on the farms of Illinois. They didn't want us to forget our heritage. I think they also wanted us to know what real work was about. Getting up early and working all day on a farm almost guarantees that a teen will study hard and go to college so he won't ever have to work that hard again. My great uncle Harvey never married, but he loved us kids. He would do his part to impart his wisdom to us on our visits. His wisdom had a way of sticking.

Later in life, I tried to sign him up as my resident

Prairie Farm Consultant, but he humbly refused. He since has passed away, but here's a taste of his consolidated wisdom brought together in one conversation.

Dr. Paulson: Have things really changed here in Kirkland?

Harvey: Fancier maybe, but not that different. It's the same land, but now we got experts helping us. Them experts are just like storms; they blow in, blow hard, and blow out.

Dr. Paulson: Don't they make it easier?

Harvey: Today, they say, "Cows give milk." In my day, cows didn't *give milk*; you had to work to take it. Oh, sure. I have to admit experts have taught me a thing or two. Don't want to be like old man Benson. When they brought the first car into town, we all came over to see it. They had the darndest time cranking it up. Old Benson would say, "It ain't gonna start." Kept saying it to anyone who'd listen. Soon as it started and they hopped in, he changed his tune—"They'll never stop that thing!" Some changes are for the good, but not all changes are. We need

"Cows did't give milk; you had to work to take it."

some of that technology but we still have to depend on each other in the tough times. I learned from watching Hereford cattle. When the tough winter storms come, they don't scatter, go downwind, and freeze. No, they head into the wind, stand shoulder to shoulder with their heads down, and face what the storm has to throw their way. Those Herefords taught me my first law of life: Just face together what storms life throws your way.

Dr. Paulson: You knew that working hard and pulling together paid off, but you also had your faith.

Harvey: Darn right I believe in God, but I never used him as a crutch. God still expects His children to work. When Pastor Olson came out and saw my fields of corn and my pasture full of some of the best milk cows in

"When one person calls you a horse's ass, don't worry about it. When four people do, go out and buy a saddle!"

Illinois, he said, "My, God has been good to you!" I shot right back, "You're right, but you should have seen this place before I helped God out."

Dr. Paulson: You're a character! How do you stay so sharp?

Harvey: The best way to become an old dog is to stop doing new tricks. I plan on enjoying the ride all the way to the end. In fact, just bought a new car. One of the kids asked me, "Why'd you buy that new car?" I told him quick as a whip, "It's hard to buy one when you're dead!"

Dr. Paulson: You're one of the few of your generation left.

Harvey: They're still with me. Willard, Amandus, Caleb—they're with me every time I think of them. They'd help you when you needed it. They'd kick you when you needed to listen. I've tried to live by my second law:

"When one person calls you a horse's ass, don't worry about it. When four people do, go out and buy a saddle!" They helped me buy my share of saddles in my day, and I learned from every one of them. We didn't whine to Washington for subsidies. You had to grow what people would buy. You either adjusted or you starved. That's my third law: "If the horse is dead, get off it."

Dr. Paulson: How did you find the next horse?

Harvey: In the early days, you watched the markets like a hawk. The train to Chicago used to stop in Kirkland. You'd hang out at the cafe, and you'd listen. And then we'd act on my fourth law: "It's easiest to ride a horse in

"When the horse is dead get off it."

the direction it's going." We just hopped on the strongest horse and road it. We even grew marijuana! Didn't call it that.

We used it for hemp during the war. We grew it, but never smoked it. We left that to you Californians. Well, I better get going. Got to wax the car. I want it to last.

Dr. Paulson: Why don't you wait until it's cooler?

Harvey: Mark Twain gave me my fifth law: "If you have to swallow a frog, don't look at it too long." By the way, sorry I can't be your consultant. I've only got five laws. There's not enough money in five laws. Maybe when I have ten…

The Power of a Page

"You need clarity on your own non-negotiables. You need to know what you won't budge on, or you'll be buffeted by the winds." –Curtis R. Berrien

Every relationship has a beginning.

The heat hit me as I came down the steps from my plane. Taxis and limos were lined up along the road. Cabo San Lucas was a famous resort destination, but you wouldn't know it from the airport. I headed for the man with a sign bearing my name, "Paulson." There couldn't be that many Paulsons; it was a small plane at a small airport. We grabbed my luggage and headed for his limo.

Limos always bothered me. It was probably my Midwestern roots, but taking a limo always seemed pretentious to me. After all, though, I was here to speak to CEOs. I guess it went with the territory.

As the limo driver opened the door for me, I noticed another man sitting on the far side of the backseat. "Greetings," I said quickly as I slid into the leather seat next to him.

"You must be the speaker," he said.

"Does it show?" I asked. "I mean, rented lips!"

"No, I just know all the CEOs, and I don't know you.

So I figure you must be the speaker."

"I am," I replied as I introduced myself.

"Russ Walden here," the man replied.

"Nice to meet you, Russ," I shook his hand as the limo pulled out and headed for the resort.

"We are tough on speakers," Russ continued.

Part of me was wondering whether I should ask the driver to turn around, but there seemed no malice in his voice—just a certain playfulness. I assumed he was a *banter person*; he wouldn't respect me until he had tested me.

"I'm tough on people who are tough on me," I said with a matching expression, pausing for effect. "In fact, you're looking more and more like my first volunteer."

A smile formed on his lips, and I matched it.

"I like you better now," Russ said. "I don't want to be one of your *volunteers!*"

The resort was a lot better than the airport. The questions and interaction with the CEOs just made my presentation that much more engaging for all involved. The evaluations were strong and the beach inviting, but, as often happens to speakers, I had to catch a plane for another presentation.

As they were taking my bags to the limo, Russ came up to me and asked if he could ride with me to the airport.

"Why, sure," I replied. "Do you want to test me some more?"

"In a way," Russ answered. "I want to talk to you about some of the things you said this morning. I picked up a couple of...what did you call them? *Keepers!* I just wanted to dialogue with you a bit to see if I liked them as much as I thought."

"Fine, I'd love that," I said. "But you are going to miss golf."

"You haven't seen me play golf," Russ said playfully. "It's better for me, my team, and the course if I never appear out there."

"I understand," I said. "Hop in."

My ride back to the airport with Russ was memorable. I don't remember which *Keepers* he had learned from my program. That part of the conversation faded quickly. After all, as a professional speaker, I've had many conversations with people impacted by something I had said. That's my job. But on that ride back to the plane, Russ impacted me.

"I have what I call *my page*," Russ said, pulling out a piece of paper that he had in his pocket.

"What's on your page?" I asked.

"It's a collection of mostly true and mostly plagiarized statements about the principles I use in leading people," Russ explained.

"One page?"

"I figure that if I can't write on one page what I stand for in leadership, I doubt whether I would ever use it," Russ continued. "Now, all our leaders work from the same page. We keep a second page of things that might make it onto our page but haven't yet. I'm thinking of adding some of the things you said today to that page."

"That's quite an honor," I replied.

"You see, we do change the page occasionally," Russ said. "But we don't do that lightly. Because when we put something new on the page, we have to take something else off. That's never easy to do."

"How do you use this page?" I asked, now holding it and reading some of the statements as he continued.

"Whenever we hire someone," Russ said, "after we've decided that they fit and have the skills we need, we hand them a copy of *our page*. We tell them that we're going to

"If I can't write on one page what I stand for in leadership, I doubt whether I would ever use it."

offer them the job, but that we want them to take a night to think about it. We let them know that anyone working in our company deserves to know the principles we use in making our decisions. They don't have to agree with every item, but they need to know that we expect them to treat these principles as nonnegotiables as long as they work here. That's why we give them a night to think about it. We all want their commitment."

"Do they have any say about what is on the page?" I asked.

"As much as any of our leaders do," Russ continued. "We have changed the page at times. Some leaders have helped make refinements to the statements. Some have suggested better ones that we now have included, but we don't change it often. These are values that have defined the culture we try to create for everyone."

"How does it make a difference?" I asked, even more intrigued by the power of this one page. "Privately held values are easy to cheat on," Russ continued. "No one knows you hold them. But when you have written down your principles, when you've shared them and promised to use them as your nonnegotiables, you know people are watching. When there is clarity about what you stand for, it's easier for everyone to have the courage to take a stand. I know that's how I feel every time I face a tough decision."

Russ went on to talk about leaders that had long since been asked to leave the company because they refused to honor the nonnegotiable values expressed.

Russ has since retired, but the page he gave me that day has been a treasure I have shared many times with other leaders in search of a meaningful compass in these changing and challenging times.

Russ Walden's list of mostly true & mostly plagiarized thoughts on the management process (in no particular order):

❖ *Weak leadership will destroy the finest strategy, while forceful execution of even a poor strategy can often bring victory. (Sun Tzu, 400 BC)*

❖   *Authority to manage is delegated downward; the right to lead is delegated upward.*

❖   *A person may be appointed to a high position, but*

never to leadership. Leaders are effective only through the authority conferred on them by those upon whom they depend for results.

❖ *Leaders produce consent; others seek consensus.*

❖ *Manage a business by its economics, not by the accounting numbers.*

❖ *It is better to be approximately right than precisely wrong.*

❖ *Ethics are nonnegotiable.*

❖ *The personal dignity of each individual is inviolate. A manager who often breaks this rule will eventually self-destruct, but I will probably get him (or her) first.*

❖ *As a manager, ask yourself, "How would I like it if my boss treated me the way I treat those who work for me?" If you are unsure, read Luke 6:31.*

❖ *Authority is not inherently useful, but you can greatly influence most of the things which you cannot directly control. A manager without influence is a contradiction in terms.*

❖ *Create real values and the earnings will follow.*

❖   *Never sacrifice tomorrow's values for today's reportable earnings.*

❖   *Spend your time with people who contribute to your energies; avoid those who drain them.*

❖   *A person has a right to know the significance of his work.*

❖   *We will only do things of which we can be proud. If our people are ashamed of a project it will be a disaster.*

❖   *If you aren't having fun in your work, fix the problem before it becomes serious; ask for help if you need it. If you can't fix it and won't ask for help, please go away before you spoil the fun for the rest of us.*

❖   *Never let well enough alone. (Just because it isn't broke doesn't mean it can't be better.)*

❖   *Build some regular customer contact into the job of every person in the company.*

❖   *Defending yesterday is far more risky than making tomorrow.*

❖   *Manners are the lubricating oil of organizations. (Peter Drucker)*

I got on the plane, took my seat and pulled out a blank sheet of paper. One question drove me, "What would I put on *my page?*"

Honor is a gift you give yourself, your people and

What core values would you put on your page?

those you serve. What core values would you want on your page?

As you live your values, take heart in the words of Mark Twain, "Always do what is right. It will gratify most of the people, and astound the rest."

The $100 Challenge

"We all make mistakes. But what really makes mistakes expensive is not admitting them right away. Business culture teaches us never to admit to our mistakes but to bury them instead or to blame someone else." –Katie Paine, Founder and CEO of the Delahaye Group

Although the pursuit of perfect products and services remains a worthy goal, in our rapidly changing world it's a goal that will *never* be fully reached. The only places that perfect people exist are in educational movies; that's because they have a script and can practice it until they get it right. In the real world, while you and your team pursue perfection, you are also expected to take quantum leaps into a world without any roadmaps. Such adventures result in a few wrong turns.

There is a second danger for those pursuing perfection. Many are so concerned about doing things perfectly that they settle for perfecting outdated processes and wait too long to embrace innovative, transformational change. Candor and the ability to admit mistakes is a true sign of effective leadership in a high performance culture.

Every change involves early errors. Catching these errors early and making necessary course-corrections in response to those errors helps make progress possible.

Trying to avoid making those errors or hiding the errors that do result can hasten the demise of even successful organizations.

After attending one of my programs, one CEO from South Carolina found a way to put the importance of confronting problems quickly into practice in a very unique way.

"You talked about the importance of surfacing errors and learning from them, and I realized that we just weren't building a culture that was doing that," he confessed. "I also realized that unless I took a risk from the top it wasn't going to happen."

"That's exactly what we discussed," I replied, proud of his resolve to actually make a difference with what he had learned.

"We have regular meetings, and I decided to throw my team a constructive curve," he said with a smile in his voice. "I waited until we had taken care of most of

The only places that perfect people exist are in educational movies.

the critical items on the agenda, and then put $100 on the table. I shared with the executive team a mistake I had made during contact with a customer. My comments had proven difficult for the national sales team to recover from. We lost a lot of money because of my offhand remarks, and I wanted them to learn from my mistake. I told them that we didn't need to lose that money twice."

"What was their reaction?" I asked.

"Some of them were well aware of my mistake, and some of them weren't," he continued. "I think they were just surprised that I took time at the meeting to talk about it. They were even more surprised by my follow-up challenge. I said to them, 'You're probably wondering about the $100 on the table. That's for anyone in this room who can top my mistake.'"

"That's great!" I replied. "I can imagine what was going on in their minds—a mini *Jeopardy!* 'How much should I risk? I could win $100 and lose my job!'"

"They probably were thinking that!" he confessed.

"What happened?"

"We went around the room, and each person shared a mistake in judgment that they had made and what they learned from that experience," he continued. "I

> *"The $100 is for anyone in this room who can top my mistake."*

was amazed. One of the other executives said that it was the best $100 we had invested in training in years! He was right. We learned a lot about surfacing problems and learning from them. We've been taking time to share the lessons we've learned the hard way at every meeting."

"Someone's making money here," I observed.

"Without the $100!" he replied. "That was my $100. Once was enough to make my point. I didn't want that much competition for making bigger and better mistakes!"

To quote Katie Paine again, "We all make mistakes, but what really makes mistakes expensive is not admitting to them right away." True winners in the great game of business win *and* lose more frequently than the losers, because they stay in the game.

To be successful, take the trap out of excellence by striving for quality without waiting for the perfect thought, the perfect action, or the perfect time. Let's face it—you won't even do this perfectly!

How will you make sure your team is comfortable talking about errors you all can learn from? Could your team benefit from the openness a *Mistake of the Month Award* might create?

The Off-Course Pilot

"Action is a great restorer and builder of confidence. Inaction is not only the result, but the cause, of fear. Perhaps the action you take will be successful; perhaps different action or adjustments will have to follow. But any action is better than no action at all. Make a move."
–Norman Vincent Peale

At one of many business parties I attended in the early 80s, this one was particularly memorable. One of the men attending was a pilot for a major airline and was engrossed in my comments about my work in change management. As he listened to me, he asked some insightful and pointed questions about the importance of early communication in managing change.

In the discussion that followed, he became *my* teacher, providing a model for change that I've shared many times. His name has faded from my memory, but his insights have had a lasting impact on many leaders.

"Did you know that what you're saying about managing change is very much like flying?" He asked with a sparkle in his eye.

"No, I've never made that connection."

"Did you realize that when we fly from Los Angeles

to Hawaii, 99% of the time we're off course?" he asked with surprising candor.

"No, I had no idea," I replied, suddenly concerned about the thousands of miles I fly every year. "What airline do you fly?"

"Pan Am."

"Is it just Pan Am, or are you talking about *all airlines*?"

"Every plane! It's really a trick question," he continued. "It's an engineering concept. As soon as there is movement, there is error. You're either fading slightly to the left or the right, but when new readings of direction are taken, we make a needed course correction. On an airplane,

> *"It's an engineering concept. As soon as there is movement, there is error."*

we put in the coordinates, and our autopilot makes the course corrections constantly as we move from coordinate to coordinate. So even though we are probably 99% off course, we're never far off course."

"That's a bit more reassuring," I replied, finally laughing away some of the tension.

"It's the same thing when you drive on a straight road," he continued. "Even with the straightest road and the best engineered vehicle, your hand would have to keep adjusting slightly on the wheel to stay on the road. If you don't believe me, you can try locking your hand."

"If I do, I think I'll use a company vehicle that's fully

depreciated — one we're ready to get rid of!"

"Wise move," he said, laughing. "It reminds me of the adjustments you said that we need to make when we go into the uncharted waters of organizational change. In fact, if we flew our planes the way our leaders are running our airline, we'd never get to Hawaii!"

"What do you mean?" I asked.

"Our airline is in trouble. It's no surprise. We read about it every day in the business section of the newspaper," he continued. "But that's the problem. We read more in the papers than we hear from any of our leaders. We'll have an annual meeting update and the message is always the same: 'We are in trouble after another bad year. You must improve and cut costs!' There are no weekly updates or direction in helping us make the needed course corrections—just yearly *bad news* meetings."

"That has to be frustrating," I replied. "In that kind of organization, in the absence of sound information, people make up their own."

"Exactly, the rumor mill is rampant," he shot back. "I think we're going under. If I flew my plane this way, it would be like setting a direction, turning off the autopilot and just checking where we are every hour. After an hour, we might have faded left. We check position and panic—'We're going to Bora Bora! Change direction!' In another hour, it's Alaska, then the Philippines, then the Soviet Union. Think of the fuel we would lose on such a zigzag course. By the time we were twenty-five minutes out of Honolulu, we'd have run out of fuel."

"Now, that's a problem!"

"You bet it is! We're not getting any information from our leaders that can help us make any meaningful course corrections. We're flying blind, and I'm afraid we're about to run out of fuel as a company!"

"I love your analogy," I replied. "The only ones on a plane with any meaningful data are the pilots. Like your leaders, they're sitting behind a locked door. The passengers are like far too many employees—they have no meaningful information. They're sitting in the back of the plane with nothing but Mai Tais and macadamia nuts. I can just imagine the message from the pilots when they finally confront the passengers: 'Unfortunately, due to our miscalculation and failure to make needed course corrections, we do not have enough fuel to reach Hawaii. Aloha!'"

"Exactly, that's how I feel," he almost shouted. "I'm in the back of the plane with no way to make a difference."

"I'm not done," I added. "I can hear the rest of their message: 'Now, fortunately, we have done some recalculation on the numbers, and if we can get rid of enough weight we can make it in on fumes. We need a few volunteers who are willing to jump ship.'"

"Yeah, 'We'll throw out a dinghy and give you a parachute,'" the pilot said, laughing. "'All you have to do is find that dinghy and ride it in to the islands.'"

"Oh, this is painful," I commented. "But I must confess that it breaks down in some ways. You as a pilot have an advantage that your leaders don't have—at least Hawaii is standing still. For your leaders, the competition is

"Whether you're dealing with changing markets or flying a plane, you need timely course corrections."

moving, the market is moving and customer expectations are changing. Your leaders need an even better course correction system; they're like a heat-seeking missile chasing after a plane doing evasive maneuvers."

"No matter how you look at it," he said thoughtfully, "whether you're dealing with changing markets or flying a plane, you need timely course corrections to make things work. And we're not getting the information to help us make those course adjustments."

Not long after this conversation, Pan Am did go under. I don't remember the name of my thoughtful pilot nor did I learn the outcome of his own career challenges, but his great analogy lives on whenever I speak about *making change work*.

Whenever you go through change, expect that there will be error. Hidden errors become major problems that require costly adjustments later. By confronting problems early and seeing such information as course correction data that is useful in reaching your destination, all problems become stepping stones to success.

If you want to soar on the wings of change as a leader, don't forget to build a culture that embraces early course corrections on your way to reaching *your* Hawaii!

The Drop-out Doctor

"All too often, minority kids never hear about anyone other than athletes. They don't know the living you can make with your mind. When I hear the same thing in black schools as white, kids talking about becoming doctors and lawyers, I know the ghetto will disappear."
–Rosy Grier

It seemed like just another opportunity to speak to an association. I was passing the time before the presentation talking to the engaging physician who was to introduce me. Our conversation about the association turned into a personal disclosure about his unique career path. He had become a surgeon at the seemingly late age of 49. When I commented on that fact, he smiled and confided, "It takes longer when you start out as a hospital janitor." That unlikely revelation changed our casual conversation into a magical exchange I will never forget.

Charles was part of a minority, a high school dropout in a community where if you didn't want a dead-end job, you hoped you could find a job working in the hospital, the community's single biggest employer. If you didn't, you ended up in the second biggest employer—the street gangs. Charles took an entry-level position providing janitorial services in the hospital, and he worked hard.

After three months at minimum wage, the reality of his position was sinking in. He was going nowhere fast. He saw a memo on the employee bulletin board indicating that the hospital would provide education benefits for employees. When his supervisor walked by, Charles said, "I saw this thing about a free education. Can I get that?"

"After you have been here for another three months, you'll qualify," his supervisor replied. "You're a hard worker. If you'll put in that same effort in your studies, we'll be glad to support you."

"I've been watching those guys in the white coats," Charles replied with a growing enthusiasm. "They've got it good here! I want to be one of them."

Charles smiled, saving me the embarrassment about the thoughts that went through my mind. I was wondering how I would have responded to this young man's seemingly unrealistic dream. What chances would a black high school dropout working as a janitor have of becoming a physician? Whatever my thoughts, Charles was sharing what was obviously a pivotal moment in his life, a moment where even a look could have crushed a seemingly naive, but heartfelt dream.

"I know I was lucky. My supervisor was an immigrant who had just become an American citizen," Charles added his own timely commentary. "He said with as much support and enthusiasm his face and voice would allow, 'This is a country where you can do that! But it will take a lot of classes!'"

Charles and I both laughed, partly out of the corny simplicity of the man's message, but possibly more out of an appreciation for the glaring truth of his statement.

He had made the seemingly endless steps of achieving medical mastery somehow a possibility for anyone willing to try. Charles' supervisor not only fueled his dream, he helped him get his high school equivalency, allowed him to work around his community college schedule, and

"America is a country where you can do that! But it will take a lot of classes."

introduced him to surgeons who were willing to mentor him during the tough years of medical school.

Charles wiped away the tears that formed in the corner of his eyes. His mentor and friend had died of a heart attack before Charles had finished his medical studies. Charles said with a surety I did not doubt for a moment, "If he had been alive, he would have been up there with me when I received my diploma."

As I took the stage after hearing Charles introduce me to the convention audience, I wondered why I was the one speaking. I took journeys between my own words, pulling my own mentors closer to my heart in order to feel their support and encouragement. Why don't we hear more about how the *American Dream* can still work for *all* those who live here?

More than Your Share of the Blame

*"Good leaders take more than their share of the blame
and less than their share of the credit. Bad leaders take
more than their share of the credit and less than their
share of the blame and then wonder why no one likes
working with them." –Ernest Archer*

Change brings with it the risk of failure. Too many
teams demonstrate heroic efforts in support of innovation
and then end up being blamed instead of applauded for
taking on new challenges when the attempt runs into
trouble.

When leaders don't stand up and support the efforts
of their people when the heat is on, it's no wonder that
soon they hear that all too familiar refrain—"That's not
in my job description!" The only safe projects are those
that require no innovation and no risk—those boring,
outdated but safe habits we call established practices.
You don't invent the future by limiting your teams to
following established practices.

When I discussed this point at a seminar with IT
leaders, I was approached by a participant at the next
break. His story so illustrated the point that I have told
it to countless audiences since that day.

"Your message rings true to my experience," he said.

"The best manager I ever had was the first woman I ever reported to. I was new to the organization. It was my second week on the job, and I crashed the company's entire computer system down!"

"Not a good day," I said, smiling.

"I knew I was in trouble when my screen went blank, and I heard unprintable things coming out of cubicles all around me," he confessed. "I tried everything I knew and nothing was happening. I immediately went to my boss, and said, 'I think I've made a big mistake.'"

"That took guts," I said.

"I was panicked," he replied. "My boss said supportively, 'I'm sure it is not as big as you think it is.' I shot back with eyes wide open, 'I think it could be bigger!' The whites of her eyes expanded as I told her what had happened. She asked me questions about the extent of the problems and backups. She wanted the facts. You see, she knew something that I didn't know. She reported to a *yeller!* And if the problem was really big, she was sure a storm was coming. She was preparing her response."

"Did he show up?"

"Fifteen minutes into our problem solving, he burst into the office in low-brain function," he said, trying to recreate the experience. "You know the ones who speak from the reptilian portion of the brain! His nostrils were flaring and the arteries in his neck were flapping as he let go with a torrid attack on my boss. For another fifteen minutes, he laid into that woman while I watched."

"What were you thinking?"

"As far as I was concerned, my job was history," he said, laughing. "The only positive thought I had was that at least my resume was current. With only two weeks on the job, I wouldn't even have to list it as a footnote. If I could, I would have excused myself, entered the restroom and climbed down a rope silently, never to return."

"What did your boss do?"

"She took the barrage for fifteen minutes. She could hardly get a word in edgewise," he continued. "She took the entire heat. Not once did she even mention my name. All she would have had to say to her boss was, 'Look I

> *"The only positive thought I had was that at least my resume was current."*

didn't take the system down. There he is! He's the one! He's defective!' By the time the conversation was over, my sweat had reached belt level!"

"How did the tirade end?" I asked.

"The big cheese finally said, 'This should never have happened.' My boss replied with calm assurance, 'It did happen, and I take full responsibility for this mistake. It is my area of responsibility, but every minute we're spending here is time the system is not getting back online."

"Talk about a gutsy, direct message," I said.

"Her boss didn't say a word. He didn't look at me. He just glared at her, turned around and left her office," he continued. "Now I was alone with her. In my experience, pain in organizations has a tendency of going downhill with increasing speed and severity. I was prepared for a major tongue lashing."

"What did she say?"

"For the longest time, she said nothing," he said with a smile. "In fact, she closed her eyes and sat quietly for a moment in silence. Then she smiled, opened her eyes, slowly moved to face me, and said, 'Don't do that again.'"

"Amazing!"

"I almost peed!" he laughingly confessed. "I had been in there a long time."

"What did you say?"

"I blurted out, 'I'm so sorry. I'll never do that again!' She said, 'I don't think you will. I think you'll remember this for as long as you live! Now, if it does happen again, we may have to have a different kind of conversation.' I tried to reassure her that it wouldn't be necessary."

"What else did she say?"

"She admitted that there had been proprietary changes in the system that I may not have been told about," he continued. "But then she said something that I won't ever forget. She told me, 'Most of the time I have to search to find the person responsible for a problem. After only two weeks on the job, you had the guts to come in here and take responsibility for a major problem. You're the kind of person I want working for me. Now, I'm going to need your help to get this system back up and running.'"

"What a great message!"

"There has never been anyone I have ever worked

harder for," he confessed, handing me his card. "Look at my card."

I looked at it, wondering why he was giving it to me now. "What am I supposed to see?" I asked.

"Nothing, I hope," he said smiling. "You see all that white space on the card? Every day I write in invisible ink one word: *Slave!* I would do anything for that woman."

Ever since that day, I have realized that we make leadership more difficult than it has to be. When you

> *"Most of the time I have to search to find the person responsible for a problem. After only two weeks on the job, you had the guts to come in here and take responsibility for a major problem. "*

stand up for your people in the tough times, they'll be with you when you need them. Loyalty is earned, and its impact can be powerful.

What would your people write in the white space of their business cards? What stories would they share about your loyalty and support during the tough times?

The Scrounger

"One trap—getting too much money too soon. That's the worst thing that can happen to a project.... First, it takes the pressure off. Early in the life of a project, there's no substitute for the scrounging mentality. If you don't have enough money, you have to innovate your way around problems that you otherwise simply buy your way out of. Adapt the pirate's mind-set: It's us against them! We're going to outthink, out hustle, out dream everybody, because we sure don't have the money to outspend them." –Tom Peters

Sometimes movies have a way of staying with us, enlightening us with truths that endure. One such movie has been in my top ten for decades—*The Great Escape*.

The mission of all captured soldiers was always the same. It was in the title—*escape!* It was a mission beyond themselves. Whether they were caught or killed or sent to solitary confinement after every attempt, their mission was to keep the enemy occupied guarding them or finding them. Whether they ever made it to freedom or were killed trying, their goal was to keep their guards and pursuers from being able to be used on the front lines of the war.

The story told in *The Great Escape* was based on actual historical events. The Germans, tired of the distractions of POWs, decided to put all those who had a history of trying to break out into one camp. There they would be isolated and well guarded. They would be unable to infect the other camps with their zeal to escape.

One facet of the story is a lesson in leadership. James Garner, one of the actors, played a U.S. officer. Do you remember his title? Only true fans will; he was called "The Scrounger." His job was to procure whatever was needed for the men to accomplish their mission. Whether through innovative problem solving or daring negotiations with the enemy, he was charged with getting the essential things no one else knew how to get.

Faced with the challenge of getting a camera and film to secure the needed pictures for the fake IDs, he used his stash of contraband and bartered with a German

The Scrounger's job was to procure whatever was needed for the men to accomplish their mission.

guard who had a camera and a strong love for chocolate. His masterful negotiations netted what was needed from a guard who was afraid to admit that he had been tricked.

Some challenges required more than artful sales-manship. The earth below the camp was extremely difficult to dig through. The soldiers needed picks to speed up their progress on their escape tunnels. Trading chocolate for picks seemed a bit too obvious for even a stupid guard.

Garner gathered his best thinkers into a World War II version of a mastermind group and searched for answers. They decided that axels from trucks could be used to make very effective picks. They also decided that some of the prisoners would start a fight. While the guards were distracted, men with mechanical skills went under the trucks and took off part of the axels needed from each truck. Some men were sent to solitary confinement in the "cooler," but the speed of digging increased.

There were more problems that had to be overcome to accomplish their mission. When the men got deeper into the tunnels, they found that the color of the earth beneath the surface was significantly different than the soil in the prison yard. To leave the earth under the huts would tip off the guards that tunnels were being dug. They could not risk that.

The POW masterminds went to work again. Soon one prisoner entered the room with a makeshift collection of socks, string, and soil. He used socks to store the soil; a string was used to close off the open end of the sock. The socks filled with soil were placed in the pant legs of his trousers. It was rigged so that at the proper time the string could be pulled, opening the sock and allowing the soil to exit the pants and spill onto the ground.

Soon prisoners were asking to be allowed to march and to start small gardens in the yard. The soil would be conveniently dropped into the gardens or on the field during the march. The guards were never aware of the strategy.

You may be asking yourself, "What does this story have to do with leadership?"

The story demonstrates a simple but important truth. These men had a very important mission that was beyond themselves. They eventually accomplished their goal, and they had absolutely NO BUDGET!

Large companies tend to throw money at problems. The best leaders throw focus and innovation at challenges.

Cost containment and excellence can go hand in hand when the mission is compelling enough. We could use a few *scrounger brigades* in all of our organizations. We need a few more men and women committed to a compelling

Large companies tend to throw money at problems. The best leaders throw innovation at challenges.

mission who are willing to work hard and creatively to achieve that mission.

A lot of valuable time is often wasted waiting for adequate funding that never seems to come. There is a lot of pride that comes from overcoming seemingly overwhelming obstacles on the way to success. Good *scroungers* don't wait! Would you want to have the title "Chief Scrounger" on your business card?

"Nothing inspires genius like a tight budget." Sign at the CA State Finance Department in Sacramento

Caring Enough to Say No

"You know the only people who are always sure about the proper way to raise children? Those who've never had any." –Bill Cosby

The entitlement mentality that creeps into a culture, whether it be a country or an organization, can stifle achievement and threaten its long-term viability. Achievement's power as a motivator comes from a history of earning rewards. That history is often formed early in experiences we have growing up in our families.

I had seen my son looking at car magazines, so it was not a complete surprise. After all, when the day for getting your license is in sight, what self-respecting teen is not eagerly dreaming of the car that will give him the freedom he craves? The time was right for the father-son dialogue played out daily in homes across the United States.

It was a good day, a day Sean hoped to find me in a good mood. When I walked in the front door, he wasted little time. His words hung in the air, "Dad, are you going to get me a car?"

Sean was not much for finesse; he was into being direct! His question was met by my equally direct answer, "No."

Stunned, he quickly countered. "Everybody gets a car!" he challenged.

"Sean, I don't think that's true, but even if it was true, it will now be everybody *minus one*. This will make you a leader! In fact, you can be the *designated rider*. You'll be the first in your school to not have a car. Think of what that will mean. If everybody has a car, they'll fight to have you as a passenger! I mean, who wants to ride alone?"

His face said it all—"How did I get you for a father?" But instead of voicing his feelings, he moved quickly to Plan B.

"My birthday is coming up," he prompted. "Will you give me *anything* towards my car?"

I used a line from Bill Cosby that I had saved for just such a moment, "I'll match what your friends will give you."

"That won't be much!"

"Bingo!" I said. "In fact, I'm sure matching their contributions will be well within my budget."

Now panicking as reality set in, Sean was not afraid to share his growing disappointment.

"Well, how am I going to get my car?"

"I only know four ways that are legal," I continued. "You can start your own company."

"I can't start a company!" Sean pleaded. "I'm only sixteen."

"Sean, this is America," I answered. "Seven percent of Americans own their own companies. They find something that people need and find a way to produce it better, different, or cheaper. You may not be aware of it, but there are sixteen-year-old teens who have started online companies or music groups. Some of them are millionaires. I'd love for *one of them* to be you! I could motivate you for money!"

"I wouldn't pay you," Sean countered. "I don't like your motivation."

"OK, if you don't want to start your own company, then invent something someone else can use or sell," I continued. "Write music. Write a book. Invent anything that fills a need. And if you can't think of anything to

"Everybody doesn't get a car, but even if that was true, it will now be everybody minus one."

invent, you can get into sales. Sales people are usually great at building relationships, establishing a need for clients and selling the solutions they have to meet those needs. You can make good money in sales with commissions on what you sell."

"I'm not sure I can do that," Sean replied. "I can't even sell you on buying me a car."

"You've got a point there," I said, smiling. "If none of these three options excite you, then I suggest you discover the gifts God has given you and find some way to use those gifts that serves others and gives you the income you need. You don't have to make a lot of money to be happy. I'd rather be rich than poor, but I know a lot of rich people who aren't very happy. The important thing is to find a career that gives you the satisfaction of doing something you love. Then it becomes less of a job and more of a calling."

"But, Dad, I can't do any of this quickly!" he said, as the painful truth sank in.

"You're right," I agreed. "Things happen quickly in the movies, but in the real world it takes work and time. In fact, it takes one very important habit. Far too many people make a lot of money, but they don't save any of it. I've told you many times to save money for the things you wanted, but you were always too quick to spend instead of save. Sean, I hate to say this, but you invested in the *wrong CDs!*"

There is more to the story than Sean's disappointment. Three months later, my son came to me with his plan. "I've figured out how I'm going to get my car."

"How?" I asked with a somewhat guarded smile.

"I'm going to write a book," Sean said with confidence. "You've written books, and you've made money on those books. I can do that too."

The earnest look in his eye gave me a bit of a start. As a parent, tired of the sixteen-year struggle, I was tempted

"You invested in the wrong CDs!"

to say, "It would be nice if you could start with a term paper and maybe charge a quarter!" But I knew that would be far from motivational, and as a motivational speaker, how could I say such a thing to my son? After all, underneath it all, I wanted him to be successful. If he didn't find a career or make enough money, I could be stuck with this young man for the rest of my life.

Plus, I felt a glimmer of hope that matched his own. With a smile, I asked, "OK, what is your book going to be about?"

"I'm going to write a book called *Favorite Family Lectures!*"

It hung there as if suspended in air. It penetrated my mind in stages. I managed a three-word prompt, "*Favorite Family Lectures?*"

"Yeah, you've given me so many lectures, and some of them are really good ones. They're even funny!" he continued. "I know from my friends at school that most parents don't know what to say to their kids. So I'm going to collect all the lectures you've given me, interview the kids at school to get some of their best ones, and then I'm going to put them in my book."

"I see," I said, caught up in his passionate plan.

"The book will have a great market," Sean continued. "I think parents are so busy that they don't have time to lecture anymore. This way the book could do it for them. I'm going to number the lectures so that all a parent has to do when he sends a kid to his room is to hand the kid the book and say, 'Read number 22!'"

"That will probably sell!" I confessed with a slight laugh.

"In fact, I have another idea to make it even better," he said, pausing to find the right words. "I want you to write it with me. As a father-son team, we could get a lot of interviews and you could sell a lot of books!"

"Ah, a strategic alliance," I countered. "Sure, you can partner with me. I write the book, and you get the money."

"No, I'll do the interviewing, and we'll write it together."

Three years later we had finished our first book together. Before the book was finished, Sean had already started a part-time job, saved his money, and bought a used car from his grandmother. After becoming an author for the first time, however, he did buy a better car!

He's now married to his wonderful wife, Nicole, and is working as a youth minister. We've finished writing two books together. The first, *Secrets of Life Every Teen Needs to Know*, sold more than ten thousand copies. Our second book, *Can I Have the Keys to the Car? How Parents and Teens Can Talk about the Things That Really Matter*, was written to help parents, teens, and church youth leaders make a lasting difference together.

The books remain lasting legacies we treasure, but the biggest legacy is what happened in our own relationship. As a father and son team, we had a reason to have conversations about the important things in life that few parents and teens ever get to have. We are both better for those hours of conversation about the things that matter most in life.

In an age of entitlement, it's a parent's job to empower their children to earn their own way with confidence.

For me, it all started by caring enough to say "No." You can't always give your children the biggest gifts. The best gifts are lessons earned on the backs of their own hard work.

True optimism isn't Pollyanna thinking. It's an earned attitude that comes from a track record of overcoming obstacles on the way to success. The more challenges you meet, the more maturity and trust you earn.

The same challenge faces leaders in today's organizations. They must build a performance culture

Optimism is an earned attitude that comes from a track record of covercoming obstacles.

that rewards personal responsibility and achievement. Automatic pay raises and hollow praise build entitlement cultures that can stifle once successful cultures. For success to be sustained, rewards still have to be earned the old fashioned way—by individuals and teams working hard to accomplish something worth doing.

Are you a leader who cares enough to say "No"? Are you building a culture that supports earned rewards and accountability or one that is built on entitlement?

Tough Love from the Men in Stripes

"We found that the most exciting environments—that treated people very well—are also tough as nails. There is no mumbo-jumbo....Excellent companies provide two things simultaneously: tough environments and very supportive environments." –Tom Peters

One of the reasons that conflict on and off the job can get out of hand is that we care *too much*. In our desire to avoid hurting someone's feelings, we say nothing. By saying nothing, we allow a problem to escalate out of control.

To understand how this process works, imagine the following scenario. It's a crucial playoff game: the Heat versus the Spurs. Shaquille O'Neal and Tim Duncan have been going at each other since the start of the fourth quarter. With two minutes to play and the score tied, the ball is passed to Duncan.

Duncan makes contact with Shaq, suddenly moves to his left, and then drives for the basket. Shaq reacts; moving in position to take a charge, he falls as Duncan slams into his body. Duncan's shot rolls around the rim before settling in, but the action is stopped by the referee's shrill whistle.

"Charging! No basket!" he cries.

Tim Duncan turns on his heel.

"Charging? What are you talking about?" he shouts. "He didn't have position! He was moving! Are you blind? He fouled me!"

"Now, calm down, Tim," the ref says. "There's no need to make a big thing out of this. Let's sit down on the bench for a minute and talk this through like adults.

If referees were easily intimidated,
you'd have even longer games.

I want to keep this a clean game. Shaq, Tim says you fouled him. Did you . . ."

Shaq angrily cuts him off. "I hardly touched him! It was charging all the way!"

"Now, stop this, both of you," the ref pleads. "One of you is lying. We're not resuming this game until we resolve this dispute."

Turning to the fans, the ref implores, "Now, you all saw what happened. How many of you think Duncan was charging? How many think Shaq fouled him?"

Enough! Even if you are not a sports fan, *this is not basketball.* It's more like a *Saturday Night Live* skit. In real life, sports officials know the rules and call the fouls as they see them. They don't expect their decisions to be popular. If the refs were easily intimidated by players, coaches or fans, you'd have a very long game with even more commercials!

In the great game of business, leaders are often placed

in the role of referee. Unfortunately, most don't want the job. Why? Because they hate to call the fouls! They have, however, one advantage over their black-and-white-clad counterparts. Sports officials never get to say, "Good shot!" or "Here's an extra two points for being such a good team player."

If management did nothing more than call fouls, we'd all end up with people getting more revenge than results. But when tough calls need to be made, leaders must rise to the challenge. How about when two office "stars" square off? Or when a key player chronically complains and balks about team decisions? What happens when a marginal player asks you to make exceptions? How do you handle it when corporate rightsizing requires

*The best leaders care enough to confront
and hold people accountable. They wanted to
be respected, not just liked.*

difficult layoffs? You still have to balance being "nice" with the necessity of maintaining a playing field that's fair to all involved.

Most of us have been programmed since childhood to be nice—"If you can't say anything nice, don't say anything at all." In our present age of psychological enlightenment, being nice often translates into accepting, if not condoning, the counterproductive behavior of others.

When a valued employee is undergoing a personal crisis, listening, patience, and directed counseling can often help him hold his own until he can turn things around and become a productive member of the team. Sometimes being "nice" is the best answer.

But it is equally true that leaders who are overly concerned with the feelings of others can end up being controlled by their most difficult people. The balance is caring enough to confront and support.

Like a good professional referee, you want to be respected, not just liked. Call it as you see it. Be fair but firm. Major in support, but care enough to confront and hold people accountable.

Dead Man Walking

"If you aren't fired with enthusiasm, you will be FIRED with enthusiasm." – Vince Lombardi

With recent surveys indicating that up to 25% of the American work force stay in jobs because they can't afford to lose them, it's no wonder that it is challenging for leaders to generate passion for change.

Fear of losing pensions or healthcare coverage often keeps people stuck in jobs they hate. Far too many are hoping for an early retirement, severance packages, or old age—whichever comes first. So many settle; so few find their passion.

Early in my management experience, I had a conversation with an underperforming employee. It ended up teaching me a lot about the world of work. Does it in any way ring true to your experience?

"I don't even know whether what I am about to say to you is appropriate," I confessed. "But I'm going to be honest. You don't even have to respond. I hope you do, but you may just decide to listen. Either way, I appreciate you coming in to talk with me."

He said nothing, choosing only to stare at me from his seat on the other side of my desk.

"I'm frustrated," I continued. "I know we have talked

about your performance before. I also know you're capable of doing the work. When I'm here, you do what needs to be done. When I'm not here, the work is not being completed. It's not a question of ability, but of your choice to work up to your abilities."

He chose not to comment as I paused.

"I've wracked my brain trying to come up with something I could do to motivate you, and I've tried everything I know how to do," I confessed. "I'm relatively new as a manager, so I finally realized that I might be the problem. I decided that maybe I needed to seek your advice. You've worked for many managers over the years. I'm sure you've had some that you loved working for. I'd like to know what they did as managers to help you stay excited about your work. I'm willing to learn from your experience and adjust how I deal with you. Are you aware of anything that I might do that could help?"

There was a long pause and no comment.

"OK, if it's not me, then maybe it *is* you," I asserted. I waited for a moment before continuing. "You've been doing this job for a long time. Maybe you no longer enjoy what you're doing."

"I love what I do," he said, breaking his silence with very little expression.

"It doesn't show," I said calmly. "I need someone in this position who loves what he's doing and can work independently."

Silence returned.

"I don't want to belabor this. I just want you to consider

something," I said softly. "There's no crime in not enjoying a job. The tragedy is that you stay in it. Life is too short to stay in a job you don't like. I don't want to fight you; I'd rather work with you. Think about what I've said. If this no longer is the job you would like to be in, because of me or for any other reason, then I'd rather work with you to help you find a job you *can* get excited about. In fact, as far as I'm concerned, feel free to use some of your time on this job to explore new options. I just need you to either reengage in this job or free up the space so I can find someone else."

"Are we done?" he asked. I let him go and decided that I had just engaged in another fruitless exercise in learning about management the hard way.

To my surprise, three weeks later he resigned. There were no reasons given. He just let me know that he was leaving. I accepted with controlled reserve. Alone I was ecstatic.

I'm not proud of my response, but share it to give you an indication of the frustration that I and the others on our team had been feeling. We had a going away party, and he was not even invited.

His leaving brought new opportunities. His replacement fit right in, and we were all amazed at the joy that returned to our team. Our productivity had always improved when he went on vacation; now his vacation was permanent.

I had all but forgotten him, when I received a call from his wife several months after his departure. I was concerned that she might have heard about the party. Her words quickly revealed that she had *the rest of the story,* and that it was worth hearing.

"I wanted to call and thank you for what you said to my husband," she said with heartfelt sincerity. "I know my husband is not the type of man who would do that himself."

"I'm not sure what I am being thanked for," I confessed. I had said many things to her husband and had no idea what was worth being praised for.

"A few months ago, my husband came home from work, and he was upset," she continued. "He told me that you had told him that he didn't like his job. He was livid that you could say that after all the years he had served."

"Yes, I did say that," I replied. "I remember that conversation."

"He said that you had offered to help him find another job," she continued. "I listened, and then asked him something I don't think he was prepared to answer: *'Do you like your job?'*"

He didn't respond, so I continued, "All you do is complain about it. Maybe your manager is right. He said he'd help you find another job. Why don't you take him up on your offer? I'm tired of all your complaining, too."

"Oh, two strikes with one to go!" I cringed. "Did he get bit by his dog later on that night? That was one tough day."

"No," she said, laughing. "No dog, and the cat didn't scratch him either."

"I'm sorry," I added. "I tend to get carried away. I've had those days too when people tell me things I don't want to hear. I'm just thankful for wives! They have a way of telling us men what we need to hear."

"He didn't seem to like what I said either," she confessed. "But the next day, on his own, he went to UCLA's Career Planning Center. They put him through

Life is too short to stay in a job you don't like.

a series of tests, helped him put his resume together, and encouraged him to explore various career options."

"He never told me," I said. "I think he called in sick that day, but it doesn't matter."

"Eventually he told me what he was doing, and I encouraged him," she continued. "He was nervous when he went on interviews, but he was so excited when he got his new job."

"I'm glad," I said. "I really meant what I said. I wanted him to find something he could get excited about. How's he doing?"

"He's doing wonderfully," she said with a smile in her voice. "He's happy, and I'm happy. That's why I called."

Sometimes you have to care enough to confront people. Are you allowing anyone who works for you to settle for a job they hate? No *dead men walking* need to remain in jobs they detest!

Honest feedback given in a spirit of support can be the best message you can give as a leader. Don't expect your advice to be appreciated at the time, but some people need a push to find their potential and their renewed passion.

If you need a push yourself, consider this my conversation with you. Life is just too short to stay in a job you hate!

"You can buy a man's time; you can buy his physical presence at a given place; you can even buy a measured number of his skilled muscular motions per hour. But you can not buy enthusiasm...you can not buy loyalty... you can not buy the devotion of hearts, minds, and souls. You must earn these." – Clarence Francis

My Friend the Baggage Handler

"Before you embark on a journey of revenge, dig two graves." –Confucius

On my way to catch a plane at New York's Kennedy Airport, I was waiting curbside in a long line to check my bags. The man in front of me was giving the baggage checker a difficult time. His yelling made quite a scene. Despite the angry barrage of words, the handler remained calm.

I didn't say anything—the man was not only upset, he was big! As he finally walked into the terminal, I expressed my sympathy to the checker.

"I'm sorry you had to go through that. Do people talk that way to you often?" I asked him.

"Oh, yeah. You get used to that around here," he replied.

I countered with a laugh, "Well, I don't think I'd get used to it."

"Don't worry, bud," he drawled, as he slapped the tags on my suitcases. "After all, the customer's always right!"

As a psychologist, I had a pretty good idea he didn't really mean that. "Well, I don't think he was right in this case," I countered.

"Don't worry," the checker repeated with quiet confidence and a smile. "I've already gotten even."

"What do you mean?" I asked, my eyes opening wider as I talked.

"He's going to Chicago," the man said, "but his bags are going to Japan!"

I laughed even more than was appropriate. In fact, I don't think I'd ever been friendlier to an individual in my entire life. After all, I wanted to go to LA, and I wanted my bags to go there with me. I am pleased to report that my luggage arrived with my plane, but before the flight, as I walked to my plane, I kept thinking about the incident.

Initially, I could see how the traveler deserved what he had received, but then I realized there had been moments

"He's going to Chicago, but his bags are going to Japan!"

in my life that I just might have deserved getting my own bags sent to Japan. Like me, maybe the traveler would have calmed down once he got on his plane and even felt badly about how he had treated the baggage handler.

But when our volatile business traveler arrived in Chicago and watched the carousel stop with no bags, I could see his blood pressure rising and some poor customer service agent getting his next dose of venom. I could see how the cycle of getting even might just get back to my friend, the baggage handler. Too many times we watch cycles of revenge take a heavy toll on relationships.

Some people don't get mad; they just get even. But getting even seldom works in the long run. Learn to treat every person you meet with a bit more understanding, a

Don't settle for revenge when what you really want are results.

cordial smile, and a ready sense of humor. After all, you can be a hundred percent right and still have your bags sent to Japan unless you treat people the way you would like to be treated.

Whether on or off the job, don't settle for revenge when what you really want are results. When you face frustrating encounters, try a little more courtesy and sensitivity, and you may be pleased with the results you achieve.

Getting Close to Enemies

"If everybody you invite into your life...all look just like you, why not invite a friend from a different race or ethnic group to come to your house? If we could expand the horizon of people we respect, it would take us a long way toward ending racism. You cannot dislike, distrust or hate people you respect." –Barbara Jordon, former U.S. Representative

Most of us have experienced that tough ten percent of people in our lives who we struggle to get along with on and off the job. As a speaker, I meet a lot of people. My message is fun and positive; fortunately I have had fewer than my share of tough people to handle. But there have been moments when I learned a lot about dealing with *enemies* in my midst.

I was leading a two-day retreat for top executives focused on strategic issues. The retreat was to be very interactive, and I was eager to work with the whole team. I had been warned about one participant who was not excited about attending. Having a good track record with difficult people, I was confident that I could win him over. He was the chief financial officer, and what I had to share would support his role in cost containment and strategic investing. I was sure that he would see me as an ally, but I was soon to experience how tough he would prove to be.

He came late to the session, and, with only ten people, his absence had been duly noted. When he came in, I welcomed him and told him briefly what we had tried to accomplish prior to his arrival. I continued with a short presentation on leadership issues. I noticed very little response from him to my comments; in the street vernacular, his face was "in park"!

It was not until we had moved on to isolating obstacles to their growth that he made his first comment. Writing down the comments from other members of the executive team, the flip chart was half full when I came to him.

"What obstacles do you see?" I asked.

"I don't anticipate I'm going to learn anything from this retreat," he said in a matter-of-fact tone. He glared at me. "You're too young to know anything. I have studied with the best, and this is an entire waste of a weekend!"

As a psychologist with years of training, I sensed that the man before me did not particularly appreciate me! I had no place to hide, no script to use, and no help from the rest of the executive team, who were transfixed by the tension the moment created.

"I'm as old as I can be for my age," I responded from the depth of my humor bone, "but this is not my weekend; it's yours. I'm here to facilitate and guide your time together. In fact, with the kind of background you seem to have had, I hope that you listen long enough to what we're focusing on so we can benefit from your input."

I maintained eye contact for a moment, waiting for his reply. He said nothing. I turned to the next executive, asked for his input, and then began hyperventilating!

Seriously, my mind was reeling, but I was going through the motions as I tried to regroup and write the comments from the rest of the team. Many comments and questions swirled in my brain—"Where did this guy come from?" "I have two days with this turkey!" "He can spoil this whole event; what are you going to do, Paulson?"

I remembered my favorite quote from Lincoln: "I don't like that man; I must get to know him better." But never had I experienced anyone harder to get to know. At the first break, he avoided me entirely.

Finally, by lunch I had established a plan. I knew that the buffet line would allow me to let him take a seat

*"I don't like that man; I must
get to know him better."*

before me. He got his food and took a seat. I had a feeling it was not going to be hard to sit with him; no one else seemed to like him either.

In my mind, *Jaws* music was playing in the background. This guy is mine! I grabbed my food and headed towards his table. He could see me coming, and his expression was transparent—"Oh no, he's coming *here!*"

I took the seat next to him. I had prepared my opening

line. I believe in small talk, but I don't like playing games. I had searched my memory all morning to find something that I could say authentically. I had one idea, and I used it.

"I was intrigued when you said that you had studied with the best," I said with interest. "I have never heard anyone say that. It must have been someone you really respected. Who did you study with?"

"I had the opportunity to work with Peter Drucker for six months on a project," he said with pride. "It was an experience I'll never forget."

"I've met him at a conference and read some of his books," I confessed with sincere interest. "But I've never had the opportunity to study with him. What did you learn from that experience that still impacts what you do now?"

I wanted to know, but I was not yet willing to give up my early perception of my *enemy*. I was sure there could be nothing he had actually learned, but he surprised me.

For fifteen minutes he launched into a litany of insights and quotes from Peter Drucker. I would stop eating long enough to write some of them down on my napkin. How upsetting! This man was actually making sense. He was changing in front of my very eyes. He was animated and his eyes sparkled. I thought to myself, "I might come to like this guy."

As the conversation continued, he paused and confessed, "Terry, I need to apologize for what I said earlier."

"That's OK, turkey!" I said, trying to make light of the encounter. "I'm sorry I said that."

"No, I deserved it," he responded. "What I said was inappropriate."

"Well, I'll talk to my therapist tomorrow," I replied, trying to making light of the moment.

"Before you laugh it off," he said. "Let me give you some feedback."

"Please do."

"You probably don't get many people like me, but I don't like humor," he bluntly stated.

True to my nature, I laughed before replying, "Then I can see why you didn't like me. I use quite a bit of humor."

"You certainly do. I've never seen a facilitator quite like you," he said, smiling. "I'm used to people starting with a joke that means nothing, and I resent it. I hate long meetings. I hate even more weekend retreats. This program is taking me away from my family. I'm missing my daughter's game today. And what do I see on the wall when I come in but a cartoon! I'm giving up my weekend to see a cartoon. I was annoyed."

"I can understand that," I said. "I didn't start with a cartoon. I had started by...."

"No, I realize that now," he said shaking off my comment. "I realize it's how you do what you do, and you're good at it. You deliver a lot of your teaching points with humor. I will remember them well. By lunchtime, I realized that you had a lot to say. I'm glad we've had this time to talk. Next time you speak, recognize that you may have someone in your audience like me. Don't start with just humor. Add some of your great substance, and then, even people like me may warm up to your very effective use of humor."

"That's good feedback," I said. "That's a true *KEEPER!*"

By the time our lunch was over, I had a new colleague on my team. He went to the restroom before the program started. When he left the table, the president of the organization came over to join me. He was pleased, yet curious.

"What did you do?" he asked. "I thought this whole retreat was blowing up on us, and then I watched you two over lunch. Did you pay him?"

"No," I replied. "I was concerned as well. That's why I wanted some time with him. We had a great conversation about Peter Drucker and shared some great insights."

When we returned to the session, it was my turn to return the favor to my newfound *friend*. His comments earlier had alienated him from many on the team. The man who had recommended me for the retreat was the most upset. His colleague had all but called me incompetent, and that didn't say much about his recommendation.

My goal was clear. I needed to bring this CFO back into the good graces of his team. I knew how, and I started the session with an important tangent.

"Jim," I said, getting the man's attention. "Would you mind if I listed some of those quotes from Peter Drucker that we discussed over lunch? They fit perfectly into what we need to focus on for the afternoon."

"Certainly," he said, giving me permission to use his insights.

As I wrote the quotes on a blank transparency for the group, I could see Jim turn to his neighbor, the man who had referred me.

"You know," I heard him observe, "he really is pretty good."

Oh, how right Lincoln was. You don't win *enemies* over from a distance! In fact, some of the most difficult people you know, once approached, may have insights and truths you need to hear. Do you have any *enemies* you need to get to know?

At your next meeting, get out of your comfort zone by sitting with anyone you have had difficulty with. Even if it doesn't work, think of the pain you inflicted on your *enemy*. After all, your *enemy* had to sit with *you!*

Someone Important Is Here!

"Some teachers shine a light that allows growth to flourish, while others cast a shadow under which seedlings die." –Parker J. Palmer, Let Your Life Speak

After speaking to middle managers on leadership at IBM's Armonk training center, I was approached by a manager who felt compelled to share a pivotal story about true leadership.

"You said how critical it is to believe in your people—to make them feel important," he said.

"Yes, so many doubt themselves at critical times," I said, reinforcing the learning point.

"My first job with IBM was in the mail room at our corporate office when it was on Madison Avenue in downtown New York," he explained. "I was a recent immigrant from England. My job was to sort the mail."

"You've come a long way," I said, smiling.

"Sometimes it's good to be reminded of that," he continued. "Your talk reminded me of my first experience with how special that early IBM culture really was. My supervisor came up to me at the end of my first week there and handed me a letter to take up to Tom Watson's office."

"THE Tom Watson?"

"His son," he explained. "I'm not that old! Tom Watson, Jr. was the CEO when I came on board. But believe me, even I knew how important he was. My supervisor could see my hesitation, but he encouraged me to go."

"I love it!"

"I went to Mr. Watson's office and tried to hand the letter to his secretary," he continued. "She refused to take it and told me to deliver it directly to him myself. I was nervous, but I did as I was told. When I went into his office, Mr. Watson was on the phone. He smiled at me but continued to talk.

"As I awkwardly put the letter on his desk and turned to leave, he put his hand over the receiver and said, 'Just a minute. I want to talk to you.'"

"You're kidding!" I said with a smile.

"All I could think of was that I had done something *so wrong* that I was going to be fired by the head of the company after only a week," he said, laughing. "Watson ended his conversation on the phone by saying, 'I'm going to have to wrap this up, someone important is here to see me.' I remember consciously looking around the room; I was the only person there."

"What did he say?"

"He put down the phone and looked me squarely in the eyes and said, 'You're new here, aren't you?'" the manager continued. "All I could muster in my moment of panic was 'Yes.' He told me that it was his policy that every new employee in the mail room be asked to bring a letter to his office because he wanted to personally welcome them to the company."

"Now, that's making people feel important!"

"I remember his words as if it was yesterday," he continued. "Watson told me, 'Every employee is important in sustaining excellence. We expect a lot out of you. In

> *"Someone important*
> *is here to see you."*

fact, if you ever have a new idea about how to do things better, you tell your supervisor. And if he doesn't listen, you're going to see me around the company, and you tell me!"

"Amazing."

"I walked out of that office on a cloud, and I knew I wasn't going to let him down," he explained. "He believed in me and thought *I* was important. Ever since then as a manager at IBM, I have felt that it was my responsibility to live that same message of support. Today, you just reminded me again of how critical it is to make my people feel important."

Do you have any people who deserve to feel special today?

Just Who Is Important?

"No matter how busy you are, you must take time to make the other person feel important." — Mary Kay Ash

While Mary Kay Ash was still alive, I had the great fortune of hearing her speak about her early days as she launched her massive cosmetic empire. She talked about an early professional speaker who had inspired her. She had read his books and listened to his 78 records. OK, you're right—this was a *loooong* time ago!

She read that this speaker was doing an open public motivational rally in her city. She went, hoping for him to sign her copy of his book. She waited in line after the program along with hundreds of others.

As she waited, she noted a disturbing habit. Some people were hurried along with a quick handshake. Others received far more time. The speaker seemed to be looking for influential people in the line. At times, he would make eye contact with them. She wondered how he would respond to her; she had no credentials.

When it came to her time with the author, he tried to move her along. When she asked him to sign her book, he hurriedly grabbed the book and wrote a note that made no sense at all. As she looked at the note and looked back at the speaker, she paused. She said to herself that if she ever became *somebody*, she would never do that to them.

Mary Kay Ash had long since become *somebody*. Mary Kay Cosmetics was a growing success with plenty of very successful women small-business owners driving distinctive pink Cadillacs.

You can tell a lot about what drives a leader by the sayings they hang in their office or put on their desk. Mary Kay Ash had a small sign on her desk that read:"Pretend that every single person you meet has a sign around her neck that says, 'Make me feel important.'"

Mary Kay talked about that sign. She added a promise, "If you live those words, not only will you succeed in sales, you will succeed in life."

Instead of being impressed with her success, she was impressed with the people who were making her success

"Pretend that every single person you meet has a sign around her neck that says, 'Make me feel important.'"

possible. Some painful experiences provide lessons that can launch whole careers.

Mary Kay Ash was one such leader. We also know she was one leader who always *looked great* too!

What sayings do you have in your office and what do those sayings communicate about you as a leader? Now, who do you need to make feel important today by your focused attention?

Put Your Calendar
Where Your Love Is

"The trouble with the rat race is that even if you win, you're still a rat." –Lily Tomlin

As a person who loved his career, I was trapped, and a part of me knew it. Yet getting out of a trap I enjoyed so much was hard. After all, the world told me I was successful. My life was working, but it was working in overdrive, and I didn't know how to find an off-ramp.

At that time in my life, I was a successful professional speaker. At my best and worst, I was speaking well over a hundred times a year wherever I was invited. If there was a date available and an organization wanted me, I was ready and willing to help its leaders and workers make change work. I was making a difference for audiences as well as for our family's bottom line. But something was wrong. There were no vacations, no breaks, and little time with my son and my wife.

I had been on the road for over a week. I was ready to be home. I found my car in the airport parking lot, threw in my luggage, and put my mind on autopilot—"TP, drive home!"

My wife let me put my things away, a nice touch in retrospect. But as I walked down the stairway and into the family room, she said that she needed to talk with me. I recognized her tone as serious and thoughtful, so I took a seat.

"I've struggled with what I am going to say to you for a long time," she said gently, but anyone listening would have known that I was in some kind of trouble.

"I know how much you love what you do," she said with feeling, choosing her words carefully. "In fact, few people I know love what they do as much as you do. I also know you make a difference to the people you talk to. I read some of the letters; you touch people's lives. But I didn't marry you not to see you."

It was difficult to hear, but her words rang true to me. I loved what I was doing, but I was gradually burning myself out and taking my family with me.

There were many feelings expressed between us. There were tears and moments of silence. Humor had been one of the gifts that we shared in our marriage. That night it was no different.

"At least you're saying you still want me here," I finally added. "After all, you could be saying, 'You're making a lot of money, why don't you just stay out there and send that money home!'"

Thank goodness she laughed. Thank goodness we both wanted to find a way out, a way to make it work. Our conversation meandered through a valley of pain and hope, but we realized again that love must be worked, not assumed.

We finally agreed that love requires time together. It

was time to put my calendar where my love was. After all, we had made time when we were dating. Unfortunately, after the marriage, the dating stopped. We'd been there, done that! After all, we had to pay for all those dates we had paid by credit card—date now and pay later!

That night we decided to begin dating again and to purchase season tickets to the theater. We made a point of scheduling our vacations and treating them like business commitments. If someone wanted me to speak during a scheduled vacation, I would say, "I already have a commitment." The person didn't need to know what my commitment was, and I didn't need to defend or argue my choice to find balance.

I must confess that at times I've negotiated a different vacation date, but my wife always has the right of refusal. Sometimes I still give up my tickets to take care of

Love always takes work to sustain.

unplanned, urgent needs of customers or friends, but it doesn't happen often.

Our struggle for balance reminds me of a conversation I had with a man from India on a flight from New York to Los Angeles. We talked about our wives and lessons learned in our marriages. He admitted that he was at times puzzled by Americans and their search for the perfect love. He was amused by how hard we work to find someone we love, assuming that love will last once the right person is found.

Like many in India, his marriage had been arranged. He knew that there was no love to begin with, but he worked hard to make love come alive. He confided that he felt sorry for Americans who assumed that love would just last. For him, love always took work.

The work of sustaining love should show in your calendar. The people you most want to see, you have to schedule to see. The people you least want to spend time with seem to find you wherever you are.

The people you value will vary according to your interests and relationships. I play poker with seven psychologists once a month. Now, that is a poker group!

Your calendar is your creed. Make dates with the people that matter most and buy a few more tickets.

If you win, you're analyzed free for a month, and it isn't a *positive* analysis!

I also sing in the choir on Sundays at my church. I have always hoped that singing for God might help with my poker, but so far that has not proven true. But both experiences are important enough for me to make sure I now get them into my calendar. Your calendar truly is your creed; you are what you make time for.

As a leader, there is one final piece of advice that I want to share with you: take both your career and your personal relationships seriously. Buy a few more tickets to spend time with those you love and value. After all, few want on their tombstones the tribute—"He finished everything on his to-do list!"

Do you have any dates you need to make and put into your calendar?

"Someone who works, has a family and goes bowling with a group has an edge on a person whose life is work. With each added relationship you have, the less likely you are to become ill." –Sheldon Cohen, Carnegie-Mellon University researcher

Epilogue

"There is nothing more powerful than story. Step into my 'once upon a time....' When you can relate to my story, we connect." –Patrick Horton, PhD

The stories do not end here. Hopefully, this book unleashes a thirst for more and will launch you into an appreciation of the power of story as a leader. Leaders throughout history have always known the power of good stories. The Biblical King David used story and music to take a ragtag bunch of nomads and shape them into a powerful nation. His Psalms were shared from generation to generation to sustain a people and their faith. Jesus used parable as his primary method of teaching his disciples and impacting the people he met.

In short, what do your people want to hear? They want you to tell them a story. The future belongs to the storytellers. Storytellers connect to audiences through an exchange of experiences. They destroy the randomness of experience and let people know that they are not alone.

The best leaders are story doctors. Bad stories and experiences hurt over and over again as people share or remember them. Good stories have the power to heal and to inspire hope. In an age of cynicism, you can help your people change dysfunctional narratives. We turn despair and feelings of powerlessness into hope by giving a different perspective. They can be healed by stories showing them the way of others who have gone before. They come to know that they too can succeed.

The greatest tasks you have are to move your people into an uncharted future, to keep hope alive and to sustain commitment for every member of your team! The most significant difference between a vision and a hallucination is the number of people who can see it. Your job is to keep telling your organization's story to create hope for sustaining a wonderful tradition into an even brighter future.

Work to find the stories that capture your vision in action and promote how the new culture is working. Your organization is like a diamond; your positive stories allow you to show its beauty one facet at a time. History is not enough. Your people deserve to know "The Rest of the Story" waiting to be told about your organization!

The difference between *being enthusiastic* and *generating enthusiasm* is whose stories you get excited about. Be as excited about the stories of others in the organization as you are about your own. The best stories capture the truth of the struggles to overcome obstacles and the hard-fought moments of victory that result. The most satisfying learning comes out of experience forged through the heat of real-world struggles. There are no free lunches, but, similar to ages past, we are all inspired by a hero's journey to success. Find yours and share them.

"I do not seek applause nor to amuse the people. I want to convince them. I often avoid a long and useless discussion by others or a laborious explanation on my own part by using a short story that illustrates my point of view." –Abraham Lincoln

When telling stories, don't forget to work the humor advantage. Humor works in ways few messages can. Use on-target humor. Instead of telling jokes to be funny, learn to look for and use humor that enhances your communication. Good humor provides pegs for retention, illustrates key points, and generates genuine enthusiasm and warmth. Before using a humorous story, don't just ask, "Is it funny?" Ask yourself: Does it work in getting my point across in a timely, tactful, and tasteful way? Will it be a bonus that moves my message along? Remember, even a good funny story can't be substituted for a good central message worth sharing.

Know the difference between *helping* and *hurting* humor. Not all humorous stories work. Avoid using jokes; use humor that comes out of actual experiences that others can relate to. Laughing *with* others doesn't reinforce stereotypes or single any group out for ridicule. On the contrary, such humor pulls us all together as we laugh at universal human foibles.

Instead of bringing people together, sarcastic humor and ethnic or gender jokes tend to keep people apart. If you must use ethnic, gender or regional humor, make it at the expense of your own ethnic group, your own gender, or your own region. Here's a handy rule of thumb: If what you say might offend someone, leave it out!

Where do your find your stories? The best stories select you. They leap out at you and tell you that they will work. Once found, practice telling your new stories to as many people as you can. Make your stories shorter and more impactful through practice. Save and share only those that have the most impact and move forward the messages you want to make. Soon, you may be writing your own collection of stories.

About the Author

Terry Paulson is a PhD psychologist, honored professional speaker, and celebrated author and storyteller. He brings knowledge, humor, and a refreshingly unique approach to every presentation he gives and each book he writes. With over thirty years of experience conducting practical and entertaining programs for such companies as AT&T, IBM, 3M, Federal Reserve Bank, HBO, KPMG, Merck, Sony, Starbucks, Verizon, Wal-Mart and hundreds of hospitals, universities, and associations, Dr. Paulson helps organizations, leaders, and teams *make change work!*

He's the author of the popular books: *They Shoot Managers, Don't They?*, *Making Humor Work*, and *50 Tips for Speaking Like a Pro*. He is an honored "Distinguished Faculty Member" for the Institute for Management Studies and a past president of both the National Speakers Association and the International Federation for Professional Speakers. He's been inducted as a lifetime member of NSA's CPAE Speakers Hall of Fame, along with Ronald Reagan, Colin Powell and Norman Vincent Peale.

With Dr. Paulson you learn and you laugh! Terry's tasteful humor and down-to-earth style have earned him a much-deserved reputation as one of the nation's best authors and keynote speakers. That is why *Business Digest* called him "the Will Rogers of management consultants." You'll understand why after reading this collection of his favorite stories.

Dr. Paulson resides and works in Agoura Hills, CA. He is a regular columnist for the *Ventura County Star* and a loud tenor in the Westlake Lutheran Church choir. Even more importantly, he is proud and grateful to be son to Homer and Ann, husband to Lorie, father to Sean and his wife Nicole and grandfather to Micah and Jeremiah.

Visit www.terrypaulson.com to learn more about Dr. Paulson's programs, resources and services. Sign up there for his biweekly e-zine on mastery and mirth. You may also want to take time to visit his blogs at http://www.MotivationLine.com and http://www.LeaderLine.net to add your comments to the timely topics and insights.

Terry L. Paulson, PhD, CSP, CPAE
Amber Eagle Press
Paulson and Associates, Inc.
Post Office Box 365
Agoura Hills, CA 91376-0365
800-521-6172; 818-991-5110
http://www.TerryPaulson.com
http://www.LeaderLine.net
http://www.MotivationLine.com
info@terrypaulson.com

Dr. Paulson's Other Books and Resources

Paulson, Terry L. *50 Tips for Speaking Like a Pro*, Thomson Learning, Boston, MA, 1999.

Paulson, Terry & Paulson, Sean. *Can I Have the Keys to the Car?* Augsburg Fortress, Minneapolis, MN, 1999.

Paulson, Terry L. *Making Humor Work*, Thomson Learning, Boston, MA, 1989.

Paulson, Terry L. *Paulson on Change*, Griffin Publishing, Glendale, CA, 1995.

Paulson, Terry L. *The Dinner: The Political Conversation Your Mother Told You Never to Have*, Amber Eagle Press, Agoura Hills, CA, 2004.

Paulson, Terry L. *They Shoot Managers Don't They?* Ten Speed Press, Berkeley, CA, 1991.

Paulson, Terry L. *Change Your Life in 30 Days*, 30-day E-mail Series, http://www.terrypaulson.com/change, 2006.

Sanborn, Mark & Paulson, Terry (eds). *Meditations for the Road Warrior*, Baker Books, Grand Rapids, MI, 2002.